SONG TITLE SERIES

GREEN
DAY

JOAN MAGUIRE

Copyright Page

New: Green Day

Author: Joan Maguire

National Library of Australia Cataloguing-in-Publication – Public entry

Author:	Maguire, Joan
Title:	Green Day / Joan Maguire
ISBN:	978-0-9808551-1-1
Series:	Song title series
Subjects:	Green Day
	Green Day (Musical group)
	Rock musicians—United States—Biography
	Rock groups—United States--Biography

Dewey Number: 781.66092

The original book was published with the assistance of Love of Books and is available through the Print on Demand network and www.songtitleseries.com

The original soft cover short story book was created and written
By Joan Maguire on 24th July 2010 ©
ISBN: 978-0-9808551-1-1

E-book re-written April 2014© and is available on www.songtitleseries.com.
EISBN: 978-0-9808551-8-0

This book was converted into large print in March 2015 ©and is available through the same distributors as the normal book or www.songtitleseries.com.
ISBN: 978-0-9941998-7-4 (large print)

DEDICATION

I would like to dedicate this book and say to thank you to my Earth Angel David and his friends, who inspire and motivate me to achieve things that I never dreamt, were possible.

INTRODUCTION

After writing the Bon Jovi Wanted Dead Or Alive book, I remembered during an interview that David mentioned Green Day and as I had never heard of them before, I researched them.

Legally I cannot use Lyrics or Music because of Copyright but I can use song titles and a total of 604 song titles (Italicized) have been used to make the story possible. Also due to the nature of my books; legally I must place a Reference and Bibliography in the back of the book.

The story is about, *Jesus of Suburbia;* an elderly gentleman who enjoys his grand children's visits and listening to them playing the board game *Minority*. On one particular day, his life is recalled in an unusual way when he gives a hitch hiker on the *road to Acceptance* a lift to town. The chain of events that happens once he has reached the town will surprise and astound you. Could this happen to our world in the coming years?

When reading this "Song Title Series" book, I hope that no disservice has been done to the band as well as their adoring fans who read it, for that was not my intention. As I may have missed a song, an album or a concert within this book I do apologize sincerely. I have created and written this story without the sanctity of the band and I hope that if they read this book, they will enjoy it as well.

Well sit back and enjoy it and don't forget that because of using the original song titles in whole, there are places in the book that I could not change to make it more comprehensible for you the reader.

ACKNOWLEDGEMENTS

I would like to thank my daughters, Jenny and Kylie for their positive but critical input in the first draft of this book. With taking their input to mind, I have improved and slightly changed this book.

I would also like to thank my son Peter and his family for their support and help in keeping me grounded.

I would like to thank Kay and Julie for their patience and understanding whilst teaching me and giving me the skills to present my unique books in the best way possible.

I would also like to thank everyone else who has helped me bring this book to life and to you for purchasing it.

OTHER BOOKS IN THE SONG TITLE SERIES

CONTENTS

THE GAME

On the outskirts of the small isolated town and in one of the suburbs of *Haushinka, Jesus of Suburbia* sat on the front porch of his old house on *Christie Road*, just a half mile down from the *road to Acceptance*. He often sat out there when the days were good and the sun was warm. He especially liked listening to all his grandchildren, who came to visit regularly, playing the game of *Minority* that was about a place called *Longview*, in his front room.

He had three children of his own, two daughters, and a son who between them gave him three grandsons and three granddaughters. His son had twins that were now six years old and the youngest of the lot.

Longview was a very isolated place *2,000 light years away* from earth, where most criminals were sent to perform no less than a *1,000 hours* of work with people who were considered to be a *bascet case*. It was quite difficult and time consuming to work with these people of all ages.

Working around the board, a player could become *St Jimmy,* a *King for a day,* a *Mechanical man, The Grouch* or a *Scumbag*. Each corner of the board occupied a different person and to become that person each player drew a name from a bag.

The person, who became *St Jimmy,* had to greet everybody who landed on one of the two designated squares, with *"Welcome to Paradise. When I come around, I expect to have brain stew with you. After a while you will know one of my lies and that is it isn't paradise here."*

The *King for the day* had the power to give you a *warning* or keep you *waiting* for his decision to your fate if you happened to land on his corner. A card would be taken from a special pile that would seal your fate and that could be anything from being shot by *21 guns,* making you an *outsider* for one round, which meant that you were not allowed to receive any rewards or get any penalties. You could even be moved back two places or moved ahead three spaces.

If you landed on the *Mechanical man* he would make you count out coffee beans and make you put *409 in your coffeemaker* or make you march as an *American idiot* in the *Macy's Day Parade* or give you an extra throw of the dice and if you rolled a double one, you could move forward an extra four paces. Again, a drawn card would seal your fate.

2

The Grouch was a *walking contradiction* because he would tell you that you'll be getting a *homecoming* party but he would *suffocate* you instead and then say "*Ha ha you're dead.*" and you would be out of the game for two rounds. If you were suffocated three times then you would be out of the game altogether.

The *Scumbag* would write a *Letterbomb* and get you to deliver it to *Emenus Sleepus* who lived down on the *Boulevard of Broken Dreams* before it exploded. There was an egg time that would time you down as you tried to pass through the maze in the centre of the board, which was never easy to conquer.

He was always amazed that usually one of the twins would be the horrible Scumbag while the other one would end up being the Saint.

The main idea of the game was to gather enough *knowledge* for you to *know your enemy* and to stop them making you *redundant*. "If I was playing the game, *the one I want* to be is *St Jimmy.*" he thought.

Listening to the grandchildren playing the game, made him think back to his *life during wartime,* when playing with *horseshoes and handgrenades* was not to be taken lightly. He remembered when he was in camp getting ready to move out and *espionage* had scattered his mates because of a *Letterbomb* being received by the *Govenator*.

"I was left all by myself to deal with the enemies *21 guns* firing at us and at the time I felt like an *American idiot*. The other company was over two miles away and it would take them nearly an hour to get to me. I hope that some of the men who are in my company will return to help me when they realize that I'm still here fighting." he thought.

The thought of a *Letterbomb* being sent to anyone at that time, brought on a *panic song* from the *last of the American girls* who were serving as nurses with the army overseas. They would fly in from wherever they were stationed and then have their *last ride in* a train and be very *uptight* until they reached their homes because they never knew if there was a bomb somewhere aboard their transport. Until then, the army would say to them "You are *stuck with me* while you are *waiting* to be medically declared fit and discharged."

One day, when he himself was stationed in another state, the citizens of *Strangeland* were travelling down any road or tack that they could find to escape from a different war that was being fought in their state.

3

They were *going to Pasalacqua* where the mayor, *Geek Stink Breath,* said he would give them food and shelter.

I remember a short private who was always humming the *American Eulogy* before shouting out *"Bab's Uvula who?"* Now what was his name again, private, private, that's it *Private Ale.* He was also the man who used to light the way for the civilian defectors with *paper lanterns.* He even helped the *sweet children* who were *hitchin' a ride* on *a jackass* or walking, to calm down and he used to give them some *sugar cookies* and pieces of cooked *chump* chops to eat because they were hungry and watered down juice or just plain water to drink.

He would tell the accompanying adults *"One of my lies* was telling the *sweet children* that *I want to be on TV* and that they would be safe."* Then he would make funny faces at them using the light of the *paper lanterns.* He was also the first soldier to shout out *"Viva La Gloria, Viva La Gloria."* when the war ended.

After the *homecoming,* I found out that many of the returned soldiers had never been *desensitized* to the killing and wounding of the innocent people so they had a *burnout* that made them a *castaway* to the other citizens who were not involved with or understood the fighting and tragedies of war. These soldiers and their families were relocated to places on the out skirts of the towns where the other citizens would not have to mingle with them.

It was not right because the soldiers fought for the freedom of the other citizens and now they were being treated as if they themselves were the enemy.

Also because of that war, there are many lonely widows living down along *The Boulevard of Broken Dreams* and their children have become a part of *the tales of another broken home.* The widows and their families were moved into a Neighborhood Community Accommodation Street that was not only cheap but where they were suppose to get support to help them with issues that my arise. The military were often not around to give them the support and many families were struggling to stay together due to the issues that they were having.

His thoughts were interrupted by his granddaughter, *Maria* asking "How many beans do I put in. Is it *16, 86* or *409 in your coffeemaker?"*

"Put two scoops in, you don't need to count them." he replied.

Then he heard "*Ha ha you're dead* again Michael. You have been killed three times now so you have to leave the game for good now so *good riddance* to you."

"Simon that's enough." said his mother "You like being a *brat* to your brother. Don't you?"

"Yep, *like a rat does cheese.*" he replied.

"I'm *warning* you. Stop doing it now or you'll get *sick of me* punishing you for it. I think that it's time to put the game away. You can finish it another day besides we will be going home shortly." said his mother.

After the whole family had had some afternoon tea, they all went off to their respective homes leaving him with a pot of stew on the stove for his supper that his eldest daughter had made for him.

CHANGING TIMES

That night whilst he was eating his *brain stew* for supper, he heard the news on the radio that the one time mayor of *Strangeland,* Mr. *Geek Stink Breath,* who was now *86* years old, was seen *going to Pasalacqua* on his own accord with *3 gangsters* in a light blue Chevrolet.

They were seen carrying something called a *bascet case,* it was neither a basket nor a case but a mixture of both, out of the back door of a sleazy hotel in the middle of the town Nowhere.

A few hours later they were then seen entering *Christian's Inferno,* a dive just across the state boarder where *blood, sex and booze* flowed freely. At closing time you could often hear a *scumbag* saying "*Give me Novacaine* on *dry ice* to take away."

Some of the people who left the dive would try *hitchin' a ride* to the *Jaded* Valley so they wouldn't be caught using Novacaine by the *F.O.D.* Agents and be sent as criminals to *Longview 2,000 light years away.*

Jesus thought "I think that the thought of having to eat *brain stew* everyday made them feel quite nauseated; however I quite like it the way that my daughter makes it."

Coming from his radio he heard "*Having a blast* with the *minority* of people of *my generation* is all I'm interested in. Even *the Judge's daughter* joins us. If she gives you *Poprocks and Coke* and it's *too much too soon,* you could get a *prosthetic head* while slouching under a *paper lantern.*" said one of the young men, who was in a group of young people interviewed after seeing Mr. *Geek Stink Breath* on the *road to Acceptance.*

Another young man said "That's right but if *she* gets *tired of waiting for you,* she'll say "*Wake me up when September ends.*"

Then she'll say "*When I come around,* I don't want any *brain stew;* instead give me either *chump* chops with chips or *Armatage shanks* with mash and peas but no matter what you give me to eat or drink I will not become your *dominated love slave.*"

6

A third young man said "Yes, *she* can be a *walking contradiction*. She acts like *the Judge's daughter;* the girl who wouldn't say *Do Da Da* to you but really *she's a rebel* in disguise and also a *shoplifter*.

If she gets caught, even though they know who her father is, the F.O.D.Agency will still send her to *Longview, 2,000 light years away* and I don't know if she could do *1,000 hours* working with a *basket case* without becoming one herself."

The first young man said "I wonder sometimes, *are we the waiting,* getting ready for a *21st century breakdown.* The kids of *my generation* are like *a rolling stone,* they like being *redundant* and *having a blast.*

Well, that is *one of my lies* that I like to tell people because there are not many employment placements available unless you are very welled trained; even the training is very hard to get and expensive for the not so rich people these days."

That news story ended and the weather prediction was sunny and warm for the next few days.

Jesus of Suburbia thought to himself "The kids of today will *burnout* quickly if they are not careful because they *castaway* a lot of their common sense. They have *no pride* in themselves any more because all they want is *blood, sex and booze.* They also want *BoA* whatever that is.

In my day, our parents would take us to *church on Sunday* and we would not have been allowed to do most of the things the young people do today. If we tried to do a few of the mild things, we would have got a good whipping and sent to bed without supper.

I am glad that my own children keep their children in line and can continue to do so in the coming years."

Then there was a news flash "A *disappearing boy* was seen leaving the *City of the Damned* just a few hours ago. He was wearing blue jeans, a green shirt with a B.C. logo on the back and black runners. He was also carrying a blue denim jacket and his hair was cropped very short.

7

His parents said that *before the lobotomy,* he became *uptight* when he heard *the angel and the jerk* talking about the *Ballad of Wilhelm Fink.* Now we are waiting to see if he goes to *Murder City* or somewhere else where he will say to someone *"Wake me up when September ends."*

This *teenage lobotomy* has left him *jaded* but not a *basket case* or an *American idiot.*

If you see this young man, please contact *J.A.R.* at the *F.O.D.* Agency. He will be returned to his quarters back in the city and will not be sent to *Longview."*

The radio station then played the *Blitzkrieg Bop* and *Jesus of Suburbia* thought to himself "Who or what do all these abbreviated names stand for? I will have to ask one of the girls the next time I see them." as he made himself a cup of coffee before settling into his comfy chair and falling into a deep sleep.

COINCIDENCES

The following morning, he woke early and was surprised to see that he had slept all night in his chair, something he rarely did. He had breakfast and did his usual chores, but somehow today was different, he felt different. He couldn't work out why or in what way, but things were different today than they were from every other day.

He had to go to town today so he got into his car that started the first time he turned the ignition key, something that had never happened before and headed off. He turned his old Dodge out of his driveway into *Christie Road,* drove down the deserted tree lined road and turned left onto the *road to Acceptance* as if he was *going to Pasalacqua;* a large town seventy miles away.

About a mile down the road he noticed a new *westbound sign* that read "*WELCOME TO PARADISE.* Holiday houses and apartments are available for sale, lease or renting on THE *BOULEVARD DE SUENOS ROTOS,* or on THE *BOULEVARD OF BROKEN DREAMS* and on THE *BOULEVARD OF BROKEN SONGS.* It doesn't matter if you have been made *redundant* lately, suffering from *burnout* or you are a *castaway* who has just returned from *Longview, 2,000 light years away. In the end* we can work out a deal for you."

Just past the sign he pulled off the road to give a young female about twenty two years of age, dressed in a denim outfit and black boots and carrying a large knapsack on her back, who was *hitchin' a ride,* a lift.

He asked her first where *she* was heading and she replied "I am heading for a place called *East Jesus Nowhere* and it is supposed to be this side of *Haushinka.* I am going there for a *deadbeat holiday* with my cousin who is a *dominated love slave. She's a rebel* and a *shoplifter,* although at times she can be a *walking contradiction.* I hope to contact my parents to tell them *we're coming home* again once I have spoken to her and talked her into it."

He told her that he could take her as far as Acceptance but he had never heard of the other places where she was heading to were, at least not around these parts.

She got into the Dodge and said "That's OK; *you're stuck with me* until we reach the town. What is your name? Mine is *Maria.*"

9

He said "My name is *Jesus of Suburbia* and how long are you going on your holiday for?"

A conversation between them began.

Maria: "I was made *redundant* lately but *I want to be on TV* as a weather girl or a reporter or a hostess of a show. I may be a bit *jaded* at the moment and I may be a *fashion victim* but I have my dreams and goals. I am not a *basket case* either; I just want to say *good riddance* to my old life. *No one knows* what the future may bring forth."

Jesus: "You are an *extraordinary girl*. Do you have a boyfriend?"

Maria: "Yes. His name is *Emenus Sleepus*. He is in one of the *minority* groups because all of the *nice guys finish last*."

Jesus thought "That name is one from the game that my grandchildren play." and then he said "what did he say about your *holiday* when you told him where you were going?"

Maria: "I never really told him the truth; I just told him *one of my lies*. His nickname for me is *platypus* and I didn't want him saying to me, *Platypus I hate you*. I ask *only of you,* that you'll stay because you're the *best thing in town* for me and I'll miss you if you leave me. I left anyway. He'll *get over it;* he usually does."

Jesus: "Did you think of *coming clean* with him when he said that?"

Maria: "I did, but he is not *desensitized* to the outside world of our home town of *Paranoia*. Like I said before, he is in one of the *minority* groups of *my generation* and if he's not careful, he will either become a *brat* or a *basket case*. I knew that if I stayed he would suffocate me; anyway he is only *16* years old and he is too young for me."

Jesus: "Acceptance is *16* miles ahead and that is where I must leave you because I have to turn off and you will need to continue on."

As they drove into the outskirts of the town, *Maria* asked him to drop her off there on the highway, so she could start *hitchin' a ride* again.

As she got out the car, it started raining and she said "*Why does it always rain on me?* Thanks for the lift and it was nice meeting you."

She walked off in the rain and tried *hitchin' a ride* again.

They exchanged their goodbyes and as he drove away, he suddenly realized again that most of the conversation they had had and the places she was trying to get too, were either part of the game *Minority* or parts of his life during wartime.

"I know that I felt different this morning and couldn't explain why but now I feel weird. I hope that I am not becoming a *basket case* myself." he thought.

IN TOWN

After driving down a busy road for about twenty minutes he reached the part of town where he was hoping to be by lunch time.

In this section of town there were a couple of supermarkets, competing for your business, a Macy's Department Store, who every year around Christmas would hold their *Macy's Day Parade* mainly for the children, a Post Office, several banks, a Library, the *DO DA DA* Café and the *Android* Hotel where he usually stayed overnight when he came to town.

There were many other stores, offices and agencies in close proximity of the Court House and Police Station that was situated next to the park, opposite the Library.

He booked himself into the hotel and went down for some lunch. On the menu for that day was *Armatage Shanks* with mash, peas and gravy, Braised *Chump* Chops with chips and ketchup and *Brain Stew* with corn bread triangles. He noticed a little further down on the menu, a cheese platter that had *Roshambo* cheese as the highlight of the dish.

It didn't take him long to make up his mind as to what he was going to eat.

"Both my favorite foods are on the menu today, *Brain Stew* and *Roshambo* cheese platter which is my all time favorite cheese; mind you it tastes just like *rotting sassafras roots* and will give you *geek stink breath,* even after brushing your teeth and chewing on strong mints, but I don't care because I like it; just *like a rat does cheese.*" he thought.

After lunch, he went for a walk around town to see if there were any new places and businesses that had either been built or had been converted or upgraded since his last visit over two months ago.

Yes, there was a new Coffee Bean store that said to get the real taste from the beans; you must put *409 in your coffeemaker*. A new clothing store called *Jinx* that had opened for anyone who was a *fashion victim* of the times. A new cinema complex showing six movies, The *Last Night On Earth, Who Wrote Holden Caulfield, Welcome To Paradise, When I Come Around, The Static Age* and *Tight Wad Hill* had also opened.

12

He thought "I might just do something different this visit; I might stay an extra day in town because I *am all by myself* and I don't have anything to rush home for. In fact I might just stay for a few days and make it a short *holiday*. I can phone my *favorite son* and get him to go around to my place and check to make sure everything is as it should be. I can also go to *church on Sunday* here if I want to.

All the time my *sweet children* keep telling me I look *jaded* and I should go away for a few days; not to *rest* but to have a different change in scenery. Just go, they say, and say *good riddance* to everything for now. Go and have the *time of your life* as there is no harm in you *having a blast* doing what you want to do occasionally.

Ok; that's settled, tomorrow I will make myself *king for a day,* it will be *one of my lies* that I will tell myself. I will go and see the movie *"Welcome To Paradise."* and then go for *food around the corner* at the *DO DA DA* Café and have the *turkey dinner*. Maybe the day after tomorrow, I will go and see the movie *"When I Come Around."*

Even after seeing those two movies I will still have time to do some leisurely walking around the park, to do some shopping and go and spend some time in the library. I am too old to rush around anymore. Well, I get told that I am too old, but I don't really feel it besides *the kids are alright* without me."

He walked back to the hotel and made the arrangements for him to stay for another four days, then he went upstairs to his room and phoned his *favorite son* to tell him of his new plans.

His son was delighted to hear the news that his father was going to make this visit to town a short holiday. He then freshened up and went back down stairs for supper. The menu hadn't changed but instead of ordering his favorite meal of *Brain Stew,* he had the Braised *Chump* Chops with chips and ketchup instead.

After his meal he went into the lounge bar where he sat, had a couple of drinks and watched *the grand final* game reply of the local football club, The Acceptance Razorbacks and The Pasalacqua *La Fata* Football Club.

He heard someone shout out "Did you see that; that's *one for the Razorbacks."*

13

"Yeah, yeah, it's the *same old shit* that they always try. They won't win because you always put a *jinx* on them with your carrying on." was the response from a different part of the room.

"No, it wasn't. That was definitely *one for the Razorbacks* and I don't put a *jinx* on them. You just *take back* what you said or else." was the reply.

"Are you *warning* me? What! Are going to make me spit out more of the *words I might have ate? When I come around* there, we will see who the *worry rock* is. When you see me and just before I hit you, you will be asking everyone in the room to *wake me up when September ends*. The next thing you'll be saying is *what's up doc?*"

"*Jesus of Suburbia,* I thought that was you. What are you doing in town?" asked a man behind him.

He turned around and saw an old friend who he hadn't seen for years. "Waba Se Wasca. Well I never, how have you been?" said Jesus.

The two old friends sat talking for a long time and decided to spend the following day together otherwise they would be walking alone around town. They even discussed *the grand final* game reply that had just finished in a draw.

It just so happened, that Waba was staying in the same hotel but on a different floor, so they arranged to have breakfast together the following morning before setting off for the day.

A RELAXING DAY

As it happened; Jesus and Waba both reached the dining room at the same time and ordered the same meal from the menu; Ham and eggs sunnyside up, toast, orange juice and black coffee.

Waba: "Now, that was a good meal. What did you intend to do today?"

Jesus: "Well, I had intended to go and see the movie *Welcome To Paradise* and then go to the *DO DA DA* Café around the corner for lunch."

Waba: "I heard that movie is supposed to be a chick flick but another friend of mine has seen it. He said that it was something about an Earth Angel David, who will put a little love in your heart and ask Venus, the Goddess of love to do the *rest*. He said that it was a good movie and if I had the chance, I should go and see it."

Jesus: "That's what I had planned for this morning and I was going to let this afternoon take care of itself. What did you have planned for today?"

Waba: "Practically the same thing but the other way around. I was going to go to the movies this afternoon but I don't exactly know what I want to see yet."

Jesus: "You got any plans for tomorrow yet?"

Waba: "Yes. I was going to see another movie *When I Come Around* and maybe afterwards go shopping. I haven't worked out times yet."

Jesus: "Well, I was going to do the same thing however I want to go to the Library before I go home. What is the reason for you coming to town this weekend?"

Waba: "Every year Macys put on a *Macy's Day Parade* around Christmas time but in a couple of days' time, they are going to put on a *Green Day* parade as well."

Jesus: "A what parade? What's that going to be about? Do you know?"

Waba: "Oh, I think it has something to do with conservation, something about saving, *money money 2020,* and trying to stop a *21st century breakdown.* I think that it would be interesting to see and I suppose that there'll be some sort of carnival afterwards."

Jesus: "Well, shall we do the movie first and then have lunch and work out what we are going to do this afternoon whether it's together or alone."

Waba: "I think that's a good idea. Let's go."

They left the hotel and arrived at the cinema complex just in time for the first sitting to watch the movie *Welcome To Paradise,* and whilst in line they over heard some teenagers tell their mothers "*We're coming home again* after the movie. We won't stay in town today because we want to spend Saturday in here watching the parade and going to the carnival afterwards. We'll catch the bus home; that way you won't have to stop what you're doing to come and pick us up. Thanks for bringing us in."

Over lunch Jesus said "That movie was good and I can see why they would call it a chick flick. Welcome to Paradise, the title alone would make you think that it would be some romantic movie that the females would want to go and watch."

Waba: "So can I. They should put a *warning* on it for the blokes.
I only know that I *don't wanna fall in love* again but I *don't wanna be lonely* either. I'll tell you a true story, *a story about a girl;* my girl, who was a bit *jaded* because she had become an *insomniac.* She had just come back from *Longview, 2,000 light years away.*"

Jesus: "Longview."

Waba: "Yes, she had spent over a *1,000 hours* working as a free nurse up there. She had looked after a person who was a *scumbag,* a child who was a *basket case,* a *brat* and a *disappearing boy.* No-one knew how he kept disappearing; but he did. Before she went to work at *Longview,* she was a beautiful *brown eyed girl;* the *best thing in town* but when she came back, she had a *burnout* and was made *redundant.*"

16

Jesus: "Oh, I'm sorry to hear that. Did she get well again?"

Waba   "No. *she's a rebel* now. She said *"You lied* to me about love." and that she was now *sick of me* and didn't want to be *stuck with me* anymore. I begged her "Please *don't leave me."* but she said *"I don't wanna know if you are lonely* and most of the time you *suffocate* me."

Then I saw a letter in her hand, you know the type that smells like *rotting* food scraps *scattered* on the ground and asked *"Who wrote Holden Caulfield?"*

Her reply was that she had.

"Why do you want him?" I asked.

She looked at me with these empty eyes and said *"I was there, I was there* and *I saw my parents kissing Santa Clause*, did you hear me; do you understand what it was like when as a young child *I saw my parents kissing Santa Clause.* I don't think you do."

Then she started crying and said *"I want to be alone."*

So I left her for a short time and went for a walk, but I came back only to find out that she was gone. She was *going to Pasalacqua* to become a *dominated love slave* by *hitchin' a ride* there. They always say that the *nice guys finish last.*

Well I was going to try and *hold on* to her but instead I said *good riddance* to her. I am not going to become a *basket case* over her.

Come on, let's go and see if we can find something fun to do."

Jesus: "I was just thinking about that character that played that Angel David, I have a feeling that I've seen him somewhere before but I can't think of where."

Waba   "Now you mention it, he does remind me of someone that I've seen in the past but I also can't remember where. For some reason, it's the blue eyes that I distinctly remember."

17

They left the café and wandered down the street doing some window shopping before walking around the park.

They stopped by the pond and watched a mother duck lead her four little ducklings into the water away from the males who were sailing their remote controlled yachts in a race around one corner of the pond.

They stopped at a coffee vendor and bought some hot chocolate and donuts and sat at a shaded table and listened to some birds singing in the nearby trees.

They spent a few peaceful hours in the park and on the way back to the hotel; they wandered past a mother scolding her child. "I told you that you had *too much too soon*. If you had just eaten half the chocolate fudge then you wouldn't feel sick in the tummy." A middle aged woman saying to her dog "Trix, come on, I'm *tired of waiting for you*." and a person sitting in the shade of a big elm tree reading the book *Welcome To Paradise*.

That evening Jesus and Waba met for the evening meal and both of them decided to try the *Armatage Shanks* with mash peas and gravy and then for desert they both had the Pumpkin Pie with cream.

There was a local band playing that night in the lounge so Jesus decided to stay and listen to them for a while, but Waba retired to his room as he had some phone calls to make and he wanted to get an early night.

AROUND TOWN

As *Jesus of Suburbia* sat near the dining room door *waiting* for Waba to join him for breakfast, he heard one of the kitchen staff calling out "Chef, how many beans?"

"Put *409 in your coffeemaker*. The menu is the same as yesterday but add apple pie and cream to it and make the *Brain Stew* the house special." said the Head Chef.

Thoughts of the previous two days came back to him.

Firstly was how he had felt different, then meeting Maria on the road and their conversation and the coincidences, with that in regards to the board game *Minority* and his past; the impulse to stay a few extra days in town and then running into Waba and that blue eyed character from the movie. Why now, after *80* years did this seem to matter to him?

He had grown up living down on *Boulevard De Suenos Rotos* and at the age of six years, his father up and left for no apparent reason. It was another saga in the *tales of a broken home,* where families fell apart, usually because the father was made *redundant* from his job and had to travel elsewhere to find work of some kind and most of the time the father never went back home or moved his family to the town where he was employed.

Then when he married, him and his wife, *the grouch,* as she became, bought the house in *Christie Road* where their children were born and raised. When his wife left the family, she said "*Good riddance* to all of you, I am going to go somewhere, where I can *have a blast.* Somewhere they will *wake me up when September ends,* so I say again, *good riddance to you all.*"

Nobody can say exactly what happened but while she was *going to Pasalacqua,* she had a *burnout,* became a *basket case* and was sent to *Longview, 2,000 light years away.* In the end she became that bad that they made her a *lifer-boring…*

"Good morning." said Waba interrupting his thoughts "Are you ready for another interesting day?"

19

They both had the same breakfast as the day before and then went to the cinema complex to watch the movie *"When I Come Around."* It was about a football team who had won one of the major championships during the early years of football and told the stories of each individual player's lives and backgrounds as they chanted *"We are the Champions, We are the Champions."* It wasn't a bad movie.

They had lunch in a new café, called *C YO YUS*. The interior was dark because with the *lights out,* there were only *paper lanterns* on each table to light the place. After a light lunch, they decided to go to the Library for the afternoon as tomorrow would be busy with the parade and shopping.

When arriving *at the library with Waba Se Wasca,* Jesus noticed a group of about *16* young people taunting another *minority* group of young people, who seemed to be *desensitized* from the taunting and were waiting for someone else to join them.

The larger group was saying things like "You don't need to be *at the library* to gain *knowledge.* Look *the angel and the jerk;* now there's a *walking contradiction. Why do you want him?* Oh look, if it ain't *Stuart and the Ave.* Go on, go inside, *good riddance.*

Oh angel, *don't leave me* just *reject* the jerk and you can come and get *stuck on me,* because you're *the one I want.* Oh, I *don't wanna fall in love;* I only want you on *dry ice."*

The minority group disappeared inside the Library and the other group moved on laughing, as Waba and Jesus followed the small group into the library.

Inside the library there were displays for four new books that had just been released, The *Disappearing Boy, Like A Rat Does Cheese, Only Of You* and *One Of My Lies.*

There was also a poster on display for the books that were going to be released next month; *The Ballad Of Wilhelm Fink, Wake Me Up When September Ends, Welcome To Paradise* and *When I Come Around.* The last two books being released next month were where the movies that they had just seen had come from. The following month's books to be released were *Who Wrote Holden Caulfield, Unforgiven* and *Words I Might Have Ate.*

Jesus thought "If *Welcome To Paradise* hasn't been released yet, then how did that person sitting in the shade of that tree reading it get a copy?" It also seems strange that the movie has been released before the book's release. Usually it's the other way around; the book comes out first followed by the movie about six months later."

They wandered through the various sections of the library, stopping at times to browse through different books. One book that caught Jesus's eye was "How to make *Paper Lanterns.*" so he took it to a table and started reading it. He hadn't gone too far into the book when he became bored with it and he then went and placed it back on the shelf. Another book about old cars caught his eye so he thumbed through it and then put it back on the shelf.

It was a really relaxing afternoon and he was getting hungry and tired. After speaking with Waba, who wanted to stay a little longer *at the library,* because he was reading a passage from the library sheets about the novel *Welcome To Paradise,* Jesus headed back to the hotel on his own.

He wandered past a few shops and did a bit of window shopping and noted in his mind a couple of stores where he would visit again tomorrow to buy gifts for his family. He was not in the mood to shop today so he kept walking until he reached his hotel and finally lay down on his bed to rest.

So much was still going through his mind; questions that he kept asking himself that he couldn't find an answer for. Like, why did he still have that same different feeling that he felt just before he left for town a few days ago, who did the movie character remind him of and where was it, that he had seen him and why after all these years did he suddenly decide to stay in town for an extra few days?

He tried to put them out of his mind by thinking about what had been the *best thing in town* so far. Was it that he gone to the movies two days in a row, something that he had never done before; not even during his teenage years or was it meeting up with Waba or was it just going to the library?

OLD ARMY BUDDIES

Both Jesus and Waba were up and out after an early breakfast.

They had decided to watch the parade that started at *East 12th Street; Downtown* and wound its way up through part of Acceptance to the park *at the library* or rather the park that was just across the road, from where the parade would finish.

They were there in plenty of time so they headed towards the Library, dodging the *sweet children* running around, but still in view of an adult. They found a good spot not too far from where they intended to be and as they were *waiting* for the parade, Jesus could hear mothers saying to their children "Stay here and *don't leave me*. If you go wandering off, you could get lost in this crowd and I can't leave the other children to go looking for you."

One child said to his mother "If this is *Macy's Day Parade,* then it means that *Santa Clause is coming to town*. But isn't it too early for that?"

His mother replied "It's Macys *Green Day* Parade which is different from the one you're thinking of. Oh look there's Aunt Sue, Uncle Lenny and Dawn, let's go join them."

Then the mother and son moved further down the road to join another group of people.

A person who was standing on the other side of where the mother and son were standing said after they had gone "*Good riddance,* that kid would have made me a *basket case* if he had kept asking questions all the time. I know that I would *suffocate* that kid if he was mine."

Now the excitement grew because the parade drew closer and when it came into view, the leading band was playing a *Country Hoedown*. Following the band was a brightly decorated float covered in different types of trees and flowers that carried the *King for a day,* who sat on a gold and scarlet throne, followed by old Mayor *Geek Stink Breath* riding a *jackass*.

He looked like an *American idiot* dressed in old torn clothes that consisted of brown pants, a red shirt and a green hat. He also wore some old worn out army boots on his feet.

22

Behind him marched the Army carrying *21 guns,* 12 bazookas and 6 flame throwers and the army band playing the *Song of the Century.*

Behind them on the *Green Day* float was a beautiful red haired *Minnesota girl* surrounded by *86 paper lanterns.* She was the Queen of the pageant and wore a corn silk colored dress and had a crown of different colored flowers on her head.

There were more and more bands, floats, marching girls and baton twirlers, and towards the end of the parade there was a float from *Strangeland* that was covered in *paper lanterns* that had another *Minnesota girl* on it and a big sign above her head that read *"Welcome to Paradise."*

He heard a comment as it went by "Hey Bob, now *she's a saint not a celebrity* and she's *the one I want."*

The last float had a *minority* group on it with signs that read "Even in a parade, *nice guys finish last."*

The parade finally ended in the park and Waba said "Let's get over there and join in the fun."

Jesus said *"Let's wait awhile.* Let the crowd disperse a little so it will be easier to join in, but you can go now if you want because you are not *stuck with me."*

In the background of the clearing crowd, Jesus heard someone humming the *American Eulogy,* and as it got closer Jesus knew who the person was and as he turned quickly he saw *Private Ale* who was also shouting *"Bab's Uvula who?"* behind him.

The person walking with him kept saying *"Johnny be good."* and Waba recognized his voice and turned suddenly to look behind him as well.

"Joe Robot. It's been a long time." said Waba as the pair of men went to walk past him.

"Waba Se Wasca, you don't seem to have changed much." said Joe "What are you up to these days?"

As they stood talking it became apparent that Joe and Waba were in the same unit during the war; very similar to the way Private Johnny Ale and himself were in, in the same unit. In the end Joe and Johnny were put in the same unit before they were discharged.

Then Johnny yelled out *"Only of you Emenus Sleepus, one of my lies. Only of you HBDCHEWFC. What's up doc,* eh! *Whatsemame."*

"Johnny be good." said Joe taking him by the arm, then added *"I was there* when *J.A.R.* of the *F.O.D.* Agency picked him up for *DUI* as he pulled out of *Christie Road* onto the *road to Acceptance* as he was *going to Pasalacqua* last year.

In his car, they found six packs of stolen *Chump* chops and asked him where he was going with them. He told them that he was taking them to a widow who lived along the *Boulevard of Broken Dreams* because she would give me *Novacaine* for them. For some reason they let Johnny go but followed him to a house down the road from where he said he was going.

Johnny was involved with *the Judge's daughter* who had *no pride* in herself and no intentions of *coming clean* herself. She would give him *Poprocks and Coke,* and sometimes she would give him *too much too soon* and that would give him a *prosthetic head."*

The Agency raided the house and that's when several people were taken into custody along with *the Judge's daughter* who was asked *"Why do you want him?"*

Her reply was *"You lied* and *when I come around* you tell me that you are *sick of me."*

"Yes, she is my skinhead, rock and roll girlfriend who likes to sing *the Simpsons Theme* and loves *pulling teeth* out of chickens." interrupted Johnny.

"The Judge's daughter was classified as a severe *basket case* and was sent to *Longview, 2,000 light years away* for the rest of her life but *I fought the law all by myself* as I have *the knowledge* in law and to *know your enemy.*

I got the *Govenator* to release Johnny into my care instead of classifying him as a *basket case* and sending him to *Longview* or making him a *castaway* and sending him to the *City of the Damned*.

He was *coming clean* until someone gave him some *brain stew* with some *Chump* chops and something bad in it. That sent him to *burnout* and now he is *coming home again* and I hope that he stays *on the wagon*.

One of my lies to get him released was that he wasn't *desensitized* before coming home when he was discharged from the Army after he witnessed the *21 guns* that were firing at you when you were on your own. *No one knows* if he will ever get rid of his *misery*.

Another *one of my lies* that I ask myself these days is "When *I fought the law*, did I have full *knowledge* of what I was doing. They always said as I was training, "*Know your enemy.*" but in this instance, Johnny really is a *basket case* and is getting worse."

Johnny started walking away saying "*The eye of the tiger, good riddance* as you're *going to Pasalacqua. Only of you. The eye of the tiger, good riddance* as you're *going to Pasalacqua.*"

Watching Johnny walking away, Joe said that he had to go "*Don't leave me. Come back.*" he shouted as he tried to catch up with Johnny.

Waba said "He had *better not come around* my place 'cos all I eat is *Chump* chops."

Jesus said that he was feeling *jaded* and wanted to go back to the hotel but Waba wanted to spend some time at the carnival before heading back to the hotel.

Once back in his room at the hotel, Jesus phoned his son and said that he was *coming home* tomorrow and if he was making supper, could he please make *Armatage Shanks* instead of *Brain Stew* or even *Chump* chops would do.

He thought "My head is reeling over all the *things I heard today* and it seems that *nice guys finish last* as is the case of Johnny Ale."

THE SERMON

Jesus of Suburbia realized it was Sunday and he always went to *church on Sunday*. I remember seeing the church of *St Jimmy* down the road, so I'll go there this morning and then do some shopping before going home.

As he entered the church, he saw that most of the congregation was more of a mature aged group, only a handful was young people. He thought "Most of these people are of *my generation* and I wonder if their parents were like my *mother Mary,* who would not allow us to miss church under any circumstance except for serious illness."

The Priest started the sermon with "*Welcome to Paradise,* God's paradise. You know, with the Lord by your side you are never *walking alone. Are we the waiting, waiting* to *see the light? Only of you, dearly beloved* people, will God be your *peacemaker.* He loves you *like a rat does cheese. Reject all American* ideas, that you will not be accepted into the Kingdom of Heaven. Through the *knowledge* of the Bible, you will *know your enemy* and then you can say *good riddance to all your sins.*

Let us sing Hymn number seven, *Nobody Likes You* If You Have *Restless Heart Syndrome.*"

They sang the hymn and then the Priest said "Last night I was informed of *the death of St Jimmy.* It seems that while helping the old mayor, *Geek Stink Breath* who was *coming clean* and had been shot in the back down on the *Boulevard of Broken Dreams;* he himself was shot by a *fashion victim* who had recently been made *redundant.*

The shooter was on the run from the Agency and was going under the bridge that was *going to Pasalacqua* after shooting the mayor, when he was apprehended by a tall blonde gentleman who held him until the Agency turned up and took him into custody.

All the people who knew St Jimmy, knew that he was the *best thing in town;* let us pray for his soul, for the Lord says that never do *nice guys finish last* in his eyes."

The service ended with Hymn number ninety eight, Lord *When I come around.*

26

He left the church and walked down to the stores at the end of the street where he started his shopping. He bought some *Chump* chops that were packed in *dry ice,* a *basket case* that was a mixture of a basket and a case, for *Maria* who was an *extraordinary girl,* for all of her art supplies and some of his favorite cheese. The assistant asked him if he like that cheese as she found it very sharp tasting and he replied "Very much so; *like a rat does cheese."*

He went into a few other stores where he bought gifts for the rest of his family and then decided to have a snack and some coffee before heading home.

On his way into a small café, he passed a couple, who were arguing and couldn't help overhearing part of their conversation.

Man:	"*You lied.* You never talk to me and tell me what you want."
Woman:	"All you want is *blood, sex and booze* and I don't want that."
Man:	"You have *no pride* in yourself anymore. You dress and act like one of those people who have just lost everything."
Woman:	"Well, you're not *stuck with me* you know. You can leave. If you change your mind then you can come around."
Man:	"But *when I come around* all you play is the *Blitzkrieg Bop* and I am beginning to hate that song now."

Jesus sat at the table and sipped the hot coffee and thought to himself "*Sometimes I don't mind* if I am by *myself* because I don't have to answer to anyone. I can do as I wish, like going to see those two movies *Welcome To Paradise* and *When I Come Around* and spend some time at the library."

He saw a group of females walking towards him dressed very elegantly, "They must be the *last of the American girls* who look like girls should." he said to himself.

He wandered back to the hotel, stopping at a few more shops to either buy something or to just browse and about an hour and a half later; he was back on the road.

The drive home was very strange because Jesus felt as if he had a passenger in his car; just like when he was going to town and gave Maria a lift, plus there were very, very few cars on the road where normally the road would have been teeming with cars and trucks travelling in both directions.

As he was turning into *Christie Road,* the street that he lived in, he heard a news flash on his car radio about an *outsider* who was a bit *jaded,* heading for *Strangeland.* A *warning* was given, not to stop if you see the *outsider hitchin' a ride* because she was very dangerous and please notify the authorities if you spot or pass her.

She was dressed in tight black pants, a baggy pink hooded jacket, black high heeled boots and she was carrying a long strapped black and pink handbag on her shoulder.

When he got out of his car, his daughter and granddaughter ran to him and said "We saw you coming up *Christie Road* and knew that you were alright. We were *numb* with fear after hearing about the *outsider* and knowing that you would have stopped to give her a lift. We were getting *tired of waiting for you* to come home and we were just about to come looking for you before calling the Agency if we couldn't find you.

Where did that blue eyed man that got out of the car with you go?"

Jesus looked at his daughter and said inquisitively "What man. I drove all the way home alone?"

Then his granddaughter whispered something to her mother whose face lit up and gently said "You are lucky dad, you came home with an angel beside you in the car."

Jesus said "I don't understand a thing that you have just said. I really do have to ask; what do the abbreviated letters of the Agency and the person who works for it mean?"

"Dad the man is *J.A.R. Jason Andrew Relva* and he operates the *F.O.D. Fuck Off and Die* Agency. That is why people can be *jaded* if the agency comes looking for you and because they will find a way to send you to *Longview* if they catch you." said his daughter.

"Thanks darling." he replied "Come inside for a cup of coffee and you can explain to me about this angel that I was supposed to have travelling home with

28

me and I will tell you about the *things I heard today* and about the rest of my short *holiday*. I also have some gifts for each you."

"Grandpa, I counted out the beans that make two scoops and did you know that every time you make coffee, you put *409 in your coffeemaker*." said Maria.

As he sat at his kitchen table, he looked at his family and thought "*The kids are alright,* they never say "*I don't wanna know if you are lonely* because they never give me a chance to be. Many times they make me feel like I am the *king for a day.*"

Now, when they go I am going to hide that game of Minority and replace it with Scrabble and Up Words. That should fix Michael and his attitude towards his brother because his brother is better at spelling than he is.

REFERENCE

EATING MY BURGERS
2000 LIGHT YEARS AWAY
ONE OF MY LIES
ONLY OF YOU
AT THE LIBRARY
WELCOME TO PARADISE
CHRISTIE ROAD
GOING TO PASALACQUA
SAME OLD SHIT
16
PAPER LANTERNS
DOMINATED LOVE SLAVE
LONG VIEW
BETTER NOT COME AROUND
DON'T LEAVE ME

KERPLUNK
2000 LIGHT YEARS AWAY
ONE FOR THE RAZORBACKS
WELCOME TO PARADISE
CHRISTIE ROAD
PRIVATE ALE
DOMINATED LOVE SLAVE
ANDROID
STRANGELAND
ONE OF MY LIES
80
NO ONE KNOWS
WHO WROTE HOLDEN CAULFIELD
WORDS I MIGHT HAVE ATE
SWEET CHILDREN
BEST THING IN TOWN
MY GENERATION

30

GREEN DAY – GREATEST HITS
DISC 1
AMERICAN IDIOT
BOULEVARD OF BROKEN DREAMS
MARIA
BASCET CASE
SUFFOCATE
BURNOUT
STUCK WITH ME
THE GROUCH
BRAIN STEW
LONGVIEW
WARNING
HITCHIN' A RIDE
WAITING
WALKING ALONE
MINORITY
TIRED OF WAITING FOR YOU
WHEN I COME AROUND
YOU LIED
ST. JIMMY
ARMATAGE SHANKS
CHURCH ON SUNDAY
J.A.R.(JASON ANDREW RELVA)
HA HA YOU'RE DEAD
ALL THE TIME
EXTRAORDINARY GIRL
WALKING CONTRADICTION
WAKE ME UP WHEN SEPTEMBER ENDS
GOOD RIDDANCE (TIME OF YOUR LIFE)
DISC 2
HOLIDAY
SHE'S A REBEL
DESENSITIZED
WELCOME TO PARADISE
BLOOD, SEX AND BOOZE
NICE GUYS FINISH LAST
BRAT
FASHION VICTIM

31

REDUNDANT
COMING CLEAN
GEEK STINK BREATH
JESUS OF SUBURBIA
KING FOR A DAY
OUTSIDER
CASTAWAY
CHUMP
JADED
SCUMBAG
EMENIUS SLEEPUS
JINX
HAUSHINKA
IN THE END
BAB'S UVULA WHO
HAVING A BLAST
POPROCKS & COKE

21ST CENTURY BREAKDOWN
SONG OF THE CENTURY
21ST CENTURY BREAKDOWN
KNOW YOUR ENEMY
VIVA LA GLORIA!
BEFORE THE LOBOTOMY
CHRISTIANS INFERNO
LAST NIGHT ON EARTH
EAST JESUS NOWHERE
PEACEMAKER
LAST OF THE AMERICAN GIRLS
MURDER CITY
VIVA LA GLORIA! (LITTLE GIRL)
RESTLESS HEART SYNDROME
HORSESHOES AND HANDGRENADES
THE STATIC AGE
21 GUNS
AMERICAN EULOGY (A. MASS HYSTERIA / B. MODERN WORLD)
SEE THE LIGHT
LIGHTS OUT

WELCOME TO PARADISE
WELCOME TO PARADISE
CHUMP
EMENIUS SLEEPUS

BURNOUT
LONG VIEW
BASCET CASE
WHEN I COME AROUND
BURNOUT
F.O.D.
PAPER LANTERRY
WELCOME TO PARADISE
I WAS THERE
CHUMP
GOING TO PASALAQUA
KNOWLEDGE
16
AT THE LIBRARY
2000 LIGHT YEARS AWAY
PRIVATE ALE
NO ONE CARES
SHE
JUDGES DAUGHTER

LIVE T IN THE PARK 2002
MARIA
LONGVIEW
HITCHIN' A RIDE
BRAIN STEW/JADED
BASKET CASE
SHE
KING FOR A DAY
SHOUT
WAITING
MINORITY
GOOD RIDDANCE (TIME OF YOUR LIFE)

LIVE AT GILMAN
LONGVIEW
WHEN I COME AROUND
DON'T LEAVE ME

LIVE USA
GOING TO PASALAQUA
CHUMP
LONGVIEW
BURNOUT
COMING CLEAN
WHEN I COME AROUND
WELCOME TO PARADISE
2000 LIGHT YEARS AWAY
BASKET CASE
ALL BY MYSELF
DOMINATED LOVE SLAVE
F.O.D.
PAPER LANTERNS
CHRISTIE ROAD
SHE
ONE OF MY LIES
ONLY OF YOU
ROAD TO ACCEPTANCE

ULTIMATE COLLECTORS
GOING TO PASALACQUA
ROAD TO ACCEPTANCE
DISAPPEARING BOY
PAPER LANTERNS
WHY DO YOU WANT HIM?
409 IN YOUR COFFEEMAKER
KNOWLEDGE
1000 HOURS
DRY ICE
ONLY OF YOU
THE ONE I WANT
2000 LIGHT YEARS AWAY
WELCOME TO PARADISE (DIFFERENT VERSION FROM DOOKIE)

34

WHO WROTE HOLDEN CAULFIELD?
WELCOME TO PARADISE (LIVE FROM JANNUS LANDING ST PETERS)
CHRISTIE ROAD
ONE OF MY LIES
ONE FOR THE RAZORBACKS
ONE OF MY LIES (LIVE FROM JANNUS LANDING ST PETERS)
SWEET CHILDREN
BEST THING IN TOWN
STRANGELAND
MY GENERATION
LONGVIEW
WELCOME TO PARADISE
COMING CLEAN
CHUMP (LIVE FROM JAPANESE BOX SET)
BASKET CASE
WHEN I COME AROUND
HAVING A BLAST
WHEN I COME AROUND (LIVE FROM SWEDEN – FROM JAPANESE
BOX SET)
GEEK STINK BREATH
STUCK WITH ME
86
BRAIN STEW/JADED
HITCHIN' A RIDE
GOOD RIDDANCE (TIME OF YOUR LIFE)
SCATTERED
UPTIGHT
REDUNDANT
NICE GUYS FINISH LAST
PROSTHETIC HEAD
NICE GUYS FINISH LAST (LIVE FROM ELECTRIC FACTORY)
MINORITY
WARNING
HOLD ON
OUTSIDER (FROM WARNING UK MAXI SINGLE)
WAITING
MACY'S DAY PARADE
FASHION VICTIM
CASTAWAY

DESENSITIZED
DO DA DA
SCUMBAG
SUFFOCATE
JOE ROBOT
MONEY MONEY 2020
ROSHAMBO
AMERICAN IDIOT
BOULEVARD OF BROKEN DREAMS
SHE'S A REBEL
SHOPLIFTER (NON LP-TRACK FOUND ON UK MAXI SINGLE)
HOLIDAY
WAKE ME UP BEFORE SEPTEMBER
LETTERBOMB
GOVENATOR (NON LP-TRACK FOUND ON UK MAXI SINGLE)
MOTHER MARY
SHE'S A SAINT NOT A CELEBRITY
KNOW YOUR ENEMY
21 GUNS

39/SMOOTH
AT THE LIBRARY WITH THE WABA SE WASCA
DON'T LEAVE ME
I WAS THERE
DISAPPEARING BOY
GREEN DAY
GOING TO PASALACQUA
16
ROAD TO ACCEPTANCE
REST
THE JUDGES DAUGHTER

SLAPPY E.P.
PAPER LANTERNS
WHY DO YOU WANT HIM?
409 IN YOUR COFFEEMAKER
KNOWLEDGE

36

1039 / SMOOTHED OUT SLAPPY HOURS
AT THE LIBRARY
DON'T LEAVE ME
I WAS THERE
DISAPPEARING BOY
GREEN DAY
GOING TO PASALACQUA
16
ROAD TO ACCEPTANCE
REST
THE JUDGE'S DAUGHTER
PAPER LANTERNS
WHY DO YOU WANT HIM?
409 IN YOUR COFFEEMAKER
KNOWLEDGE
1000 HOURS
DRY ICE
ONLY OF YOU
THE ONE I WANT
I WANT TO BE ALONE

DOOKIE
BURNOUT
HAVING A BLAST
CHUMP
LONGVIEW
WELCOME TO PARADISE
PULLING TEETH
BASKET CASE
SHE
SASSAFRAS ROOTS
WHEN I COME AROUND
COMING CLEAN
EMENIUS SLEEPUS
IN THE END
F.O.D (Fuck Off and Die)
ALL BY MYSELF

WHEN I COME AROUND
WHEN I COME AROUND (ALBUM VERSION)
SHE (LIVE)

WAITING
WAITING
MARIA

INSOMNIAC
ARMATAGE SHANKS
BRAT
STUCK WITH ME
GEEK STINK BREATH
NO PRIDE
BAB'S UVULA WHO?
86
PANIC SONG
STUART AND THE AVE.
BRAIN STEW
JADED
WESTBOUND SIGN
TIGHT WAD HILL
WALKING CONTRADICTION

FOOT IN MOUTH
GOING TO PASALACQUA
WELCOME TO PARADISE
GEEK STINK BREATH
ONE OF MY LIES
STUCK WITH ME
CHUMP
LONGVIEW
2000 LIGHT YEARS AWAY
WHEN I COME AROUND
BURNOUT
F.O.D

TUNE IN, TOKYO
CHURCH ON SUNDAY
CASTAWAY
BLOOD, SEX AND BOOZE
KING FOR A DAY
WAITING
MINORITY
MACY'S DAY PARADE

REDUNDANT / GOOD RIDDANCE (TIME Of YOUR LIFE)
REDUNDANT
GOOD RIDDANCE (TIME OF YOUR LIFE) (LP VERSION)

NIMROD
NICE GUYS FINISH LAST
HITCHIN' A RIDE
THE GROUCH
REDUNDANT
SCATTERED
ALL THE TIME
WORRY ROCK
PLATYPUS (I HATE YOU)
UPTIGHT
LAST RIDE IN
JINX
HAUSHINKA
WALKING ALONE
REJECT
TAKE BACK
KING FOR A DAY
GOOD RIDDANCE (TIME OF YOUR LIFE)
PROSTHETIC HEAD
SUFFOCATE
DO DA DA
DESENSITIZED
YOU LIED

WARNING
WARNING
BLOOD, SEX AND BOOZE
CHURCH ON SUNDAY
FASHION VICTIM
CASTAWAY
MISERY
DEADBEAT HOLIDAY
HOLD ON
JACKASS
WAITING
MINORITY
MACY'S DAY PARADE

INTERNATIONAL SUPERHITS
MARIA
POPROCKS & COKE
LONGVIEW
WELCOME TO PARADISE
BASKET CASE
WHEN I COME AROUND
SHE
J.A.R. (JASON ANDREW RELVA)
GEEK STINK BREATH
BRAIN STEW
JADED
WALKING CONTRADICTION
STUCK WITH ME
HITCHIN' A RIDE
GOOD RIDDANCE (TIME OF YOUR LIFE)
REDUNDANT
NICE GUYS FINISH LAST
MINORITY
WARNING
WAITING
MACY'S DAY PARADE

40

SHENANIGANS
SUFFOCATE
DESENSITIZED
YOU LIED
OUTSIDER
DON'T WANNA FALL IN LOVE
ESPIONAGE
I WANT TO BE ON T.V.
SCUMBAG
TIRED OF WAITING FOR YOU
SICK OF ME
ROTTING
DO DA DA
ON THE WAGON
HA HA YOU'RE DEAD

BULLET IN A BIBLE
AMERICAN IDIOT
JESUS OF SUBURBIA: I. JESUS OF SUBURBIA / II. CITY OF THE
DAMNED /
III. I DON'T CARE / IV. DEARLY BELOVED / V. TALES OF ANOTHER
BROKEN HEART
HOLIDAY
ARE WE THE WAITING
ST. JIMMY
LONGVIEW
HITCHIN' A RIDE
BRAIN STEW
BASKET CASE
KING FOR A DAY / SHOUT
WAKE ME UP WHEN SEPTEMBER ENDS
MINORITY
BOULEVARD OF BROKEN DREAMS
GOOD RIDDANCE (TIME OF YOUR LIFE)

21 GUNS
21 GUNS
FAVORITE SON

41

BOWLING BOWLING BOWLING PARKING PARKING
ARMATAGE SHANKS
BRAIN STEW
JADED
KNOWLEDGE
BASKET CASE
SHE
WALKING CONTRADICTION

GREEN DAY – LIVE TRACKS
WELCOME TO PARADISE (LIVE)
ONE OF MY LIES (LIVE)
CHUMP (LIVE)
LONGVIEW (LIVE)
BURNOUT (LIVE)
2000 LIGHT YEARS AWAY (LIVE)

HOLIDAY
HOLIDAY
MINORITY (LIVE)

AMERICAN IDIOT
JESUS OF SUBURBIA: I. JESUS OF SUBURBIA / II. CITY OF THE
DAMNED /
III. TALES OF ANOTHER BROKEN HEART
HOLIDAY
BOULEVARD OF BROKEN DREAMS
ARE WE WAITING
ST. JIMMY
GIVE ME NOVACAINE
SHE'S A REBEL
EXTRAORDINARY GIRL
LETTERBOMB
WAKE ME UP WHEN SEPTEMBER ENDS
HOMECOMING: I. THE DEATH OF ST. JIMMY / II. EAST 12TH ST. /
III COMING HOME AGAIN

42

LIVE ON AIR
409 IN YOUR COFFEEMAKER
WELCOME TO PARADISE
2000 LIGHT YEARS AWAY
THE JUDGE'S DAUGHTER
CHRISTIE ROAD
ONLY OF YOU
WHO WROTE HOLDEN CAULFIELD?
GOING TO PASALACQUA
PAPER LANTERNS
ONE OF MY LIES
COUNTRY HOEDOWN AKA DOMINATED LOVE SLAVE
F.O.D.
WORDS I MIGHT HAVE ATE

WARNING
WARNING (ALBUM VERSION)
SCUMBAG
OUTSIDER
I DON'T WANT TO KNOW IF YOU ARE LONELY

"LIVE IN TOKYO" EP- LAST NIGHT ON EARTH
21ST CENTURY BREAKDOWN
KNOW YOUR ENEMY
LAST OF THE AMERICAN GIRLS
21 GUNS
AMERICAN EULOGY
BASKET CASE
GEEK STINK BREATH

MINORITY
MINORITY
BRAT (LIVE FROM TOKYO)
86 (LIVE FROM PRAGUE)
JACKASS

AMERICAN IDIOT
AMERICAN IDIOT
TOO MUCH TOO SOON

BASKET CASE
BASKET CASE
ON THE WAGON (NON-LP TRACK)
TIRED OF WAITING FOR YOU (PREVIOUSLY UNRELEASED)
409 IN YOUR COFFEEMAKER (UNMIXED) (PREVIOUSLY
UNRELEASED)

BRAIN STEW / JADED
BRAIN STEW / JADED
DO DA DA
GOOD RIDDANCE (TIME OF YOUR LIFE)
BRAIN STEW (CLEAN RADIO FADED ENDING

LONGVIEW
LONGVIEW
GOING TO PASALACQUA (LIVE)
F.O.D. (LIVE)
CHRISTIE ROAD (LIVE)

1,000 HOURS
1,000 HOURS
DRY ICE
ONLY OF YOU
THE ONE I WANT

SWEET CHILDREN
SWEET CHILDREN
BEST THING IN TOWN
STRANGELAND
MY GENERATION (THE WHO)

REDUNDANT
REDUNDANT (RICHARD DODD MEDIUM WIDE MIX)
REJECT ALL AMERICAN (LIVE)
SHE (LIVE)

WAKE ME UP WHEN SEPTEMBER ENDS
WAKE ME UP WHEN SEPTEMBER ENDS
GIVE ME NOVACAINE

TIME OF YOUR LIFE (GOOD RIDDANCE)
TIME OF YOUR LIFE (GOOD RIDDANCE)
DESENSITIZED
ROTTING

STUCK WITH ME
STUCK WITH ME
WHEN I COME AROUND (LIVE)
JADED (LIVE)

GEEK STINK BREATH
GEEK STINK BREATH
I WANT TO BE ON TV
DON'T WANT TO FALL IN LOVE

JESUS OF SUBURBIA
JESUS OF SUBURBIA
JESUS OF SUBURBIA (RADIO EDIT)

BOULEVARD OF BROKEN DREAMS
BOULEVARD OF BROKEN DREAMS
LETTERBOMB (LIVE)

REDUNDANT / THE GROUCH (LIVE)
REDUNDANT (RICHARD DODD MEDIUM WIDE MIX)
THE GROUCH (LIVE)

HITCHIN' A RIDE
HITCHIN' A RIDE

J.A.R. (JASON ANDREW RELVA)
J.A.R. (JASON ANDREW RELVA)

THE SIMPSONS THEME
THE SIMPSONS THEME

GREEN DAY UNSORTED LYRICS
DUI (DRIVING UNDER THE INFLUENCE)
BOULEVARD DE SUENOS ROTOS
I SAW MY PARENTS KISSING SANTA CLAUSE
THINGS I HEARD TODAY
MINNESOTA GIRL
MECHANICAL MAN
WE'RE COMING HOME AGAIN
ROCK AND ROLL GIRLFRIEND
NOBODY LIKES YOU
EYE OF THE TIGER
BLITZKRIEG BOP
LIFE DURING WARTIME
THE BALLAD OF WILHELM FINK
HOMECOMING
WHATSEMAME
JOHNNY BE GOOD
TOO MUCH TOO SOON
I FOUGHT THE LAW
LIKE A RAT DOES CHEESE
FAVORITE CHEESE
WE ARE THE CHAMPIONS
THE ANGEL AND THE JERK
3 GANGSTERS
IN THE END
HAVING A BLAST
NO PRIDE
THE GRAND FINAL
WHAT'S UP DOC
SICK OF ME
THE KIDS ARE ALRIGHT
WHY DOES IT ALWAYS RAIN ON ME
STORY OF A GIRL
TURKEY DINNER
HBDCHEWFC
LIFER - BORING
SANTA CLAUSE IS COMING TO TOWN
FOOD AROUND THE CORNER
NUMB

46

GET OVER IT
BROWN EYED GIRL
GOIN' UNDER
C YO YUS
DOWNTOWN
LA FATA
SUGAR COOKIES
UNFORGIVEN
PARANOIA
MYSELF
CLOSING TIME
YES, SHE IS MY SKINHEAD
BOULEVARD OF BROKEN SONGS
SOMETIMES I DON'T MIND

BIBLIOGRAPHY

Green Day Cover Picture found on the following sites:
http://xbox360media.gamespy.com/xbox360/image/article/992/992840/rock-band-gre
http://www.game-addicts.com/wp-contents/uploads/2009/06/green-day-rockband.jpg
http://gamerant.com/wp-content/uploads/Green-Day-Rock-Band.jpg
http://www.gamestar.hu/apix_collect/0905/green-day/green-day_screenshot_2009121

Eating My Burger: http://.www.discogs.com/Green-Day-Eating-My-Burgers/release/1599202

Kerplunk: http://www.discogs.com/Green-Day-Kerplunk/release/ 2185891

Welcome To Paradise: http://www.discogs.com/Green-Day-Welcome-To-Paradise/master/194073

Green Day – Greatest Hits:http://www.discogs.com/Green-Day-Greatest-Hits/release/1965125

21st Century Breakdown: http://www.discogs.com/Green-Day-21st-Century-breakdown/release/2053945

Burnout: http://www.discogs.com/Green-Day-Burnout/release/1198731

Live At Gilman: <http://www.discogs.com/Green-Day-Live-At-Gilman-St/release/970180>

Live T In The Park 2002: http://www.discogs.com/Green-Day-Live-T-In-The-Park-2002/release/2138736

Live USA: http://www.discogs.com/Green-Day-Live-USA/release/ 1198719

Ultimate Collectors: http://www.discogs.com/Green-Day-Ultimate-Collectors-7-Vinyl-Singles-Box-Set/rele

When I Come Around: http://www.discogs.com/Green-Day-When-I-Come-Around/master/68814

39/Smooth: http://www.discogs.com/Green-Day-39Smooth/master/ 223412

1,039 / Smoothed Out Slappy Hours: http://www.discogs.com/Green-Day-1039-Smoothed-Out-Slappy-Hours/master/33155

Waiting: http://www.discogs.com/Green-Day-Waiting/master/157544

Dookie: http://www.discogs.com/Green-Day-Dookie/master/33170

Insomniac: <http://www.discogs.com/Green-Day-Insomniac/master/68787 >

Foot In Mouth: http://www.discogs.com/Green-Day-Foot-In-Mouth/release/785643

Tune In, Tokyo: http://www.discogs.com/Green-Day-Tune-In-Tokyo/release/793480

Nimrod: http://www.discogs.com/Green-Day-Nimrod/master/68804

Warning: http://www.discogs.com/Green-Day-Warning/master/68821

International Superhits: http://www.discogs.com/Green-Day-International-Superhits/master/68790

Shenanigans: <http://www.discogs.com/Green-Day-Shenanigans /master/68842>

Redundant / Good Riddance (Time Of Your Life): <http://www.discogs.com/ Green-Day-Redundant-Good-Riddance-Time-Of-Your-Life/re>

Bullet In A Bible: http://www.discogs.com/Green-Day-Bullet-In-A-Bible/master/179762

Bowling Bowling Bowling Parking Parking: <http://www.discogs.com/ Green-Day-Bowling-Bowling-Bowling-Parking-Parking/rele>

Green Day – Live Tracks: http://www.discogs.com/Green-Day-Live-Tracks/release/798805

21 Guns: http://www.discogs.com/Green-Day-21-Guns/master/157541

Holiday: http://www.discogs.com/Green-Day-2Holiday/master/151339

American Idiot: <http://www.discogs.com/Green-Day-American-Idiot
/master/33161>

Live On Air: <http://www.discogs.com/Green-Day-Live-On-Air/
release/2006400>

Warning: http://www.discogs.com/Green-Day-Warning/master/238897

Live In Tokyo" EP – Last Night On Earth: http://www.discogs.com/ Green-Day-
Live-In-Tokyo-EP-Last-Night-On-Earth/release/2

Minority: http://www.discogs.com/Green-Day-Minority/master/68797

Basket Case: <http://www.discogs.com/Green-Day-Basket-Case/master/ 68797>

Brain Stew / Jaded: http://www.discogs.com/Green-Day-Brain-Stew-
Jaded/master/68777

Longview: http://www.discogs.com/Green-Day-Longview/master/68810

1,000 Hours: http://www.discogs.com/Green-Day-1000-Hours/master/ 33149

Sweet Children: <http://www.discogs.com/Green-Day-Sweet-Children
/master/162059>

American Idiot: http://www.discogs.com/Green-Day-American-
Idiot/master/33165

Redundant: <http://www.discogs.com/Green-Day-Redundant/release/ 1971787>

Time Of Your Life (Good Riddance): http://www.discogs.com/Green-Day-Time-
Of-Your-Life-Good-Riddance/master/688319

Stuck With Me: <http://www.discogs.com/Green-Day-Stuck-With-Me
/master/89269>

Gee Stink Breath: http://www.discogs.com/Green-Day-Geek-Stink-
Breath/master/68782

Wake Me Up When September Ends:http://www.discogs.com/Green-Day-Wake-
Me-Up-When-September-Ends/release/871

Jesus Of Suburbia: http://www.discogs.com/Green-Day-Jesus-Of-Suburbia/master/68794

Boulevard Of Broken Dreams:http://www.discogs.com/Green-Day-Boulevard-Of-Broken-Dreams/master/68774

Redundant / The Grouch (Live):http://www.discogs.com/Green-Day-Redundant-The-Grouch-Live/release/2150777

Hitchin' A Ride: http://www.discogs.com/Green-Day-Hitchin'-A-Ride/release/1971746

J.A.R. (Jason Andrew Relva): http://www.discogs.com/Green-Day-JAR-Jason-Andrew-Relva/release/1742180

The Simpsons Theme: http://www.discogs.com/Green-Day-The-Simpsons-Theme/release/1069001

Know Your Enemy: http://www.discogs.com/Green-Day-Know-Your-Enemy/master/157542

Green Day Unsorted Lyrics: http://www.allthelyrics.com/lyrics/green_day

ABOUT THE AUTHOR

I was 59 years old; a mother of three very special, supportive adult children and a grandmother of three wonderful grandsons (I now have five grandchildren.) when I started writing my first book whilst watching a Bon Jovi concert DVD. (I am an avid fan, if you can call me that; crazy is more like it.)

I am glad that I listened to David Bryan because this book has really been something different for me to write and I have more respect for a different type of band than what I am used to listening to.

I write from the heart and I really enjoyed writing the book so I wrote another using a different artist, and the books kept coming to me and I kept writing them as a normal book (with a little help from above).

Because I use different artist/artists song titles I have to be very careful with Copyright so a lot of legal requirements have to be taken into consideration before publishing the books in any format. I also needed a name that would connect my books to each other; so the "Song Title Series" books began.

All my books are short stories; however it depends on how many song titles there are to be used, as to the length of the book. Some artists didn't have enough song titles on their own so I combined them with a few other artists. Other artists had that many song titles that I could have written a novel; but it would have ended up being boring.

Challenges I like, so writing books with various artists are a lot of fun and takes careful thinking.

Why should I have all the fun writing the books and not be able to share them with everyone; so I have converted them into large print books and E-Books so that you can share my fun as well.

Hopefully in the not too distant future; the books will also be available as audio books so that no-one will miss out on my fun and enjoyment of writing these unique books. I hope that you enjoy reading them.

My web site www.songtitleseries.com is the place to visit for updates of new books and a place to purchase other titles in all formats.

TESTIMONIALS

The song titles series are books that were intriguing and were hard to believe that these short stories were written within the incorporated song titles of the artists that are mentioned in the titles. I loved what I have read so far and think that anyone with an imagination and love of music as the author you will surely enjoy reading these.
L. K. Brisbane Australia.

Joan Maguire Books are very nice, I enjoy reading them so much, they are hard to put down!! Especially when she does one about Bonjovi and their songs!!! If I can say, it is worth every penny, when you buy one!!! The Books make nice presents, for a person whom loves to read!!! I can guarantee that you will LOVE these books, because I do!!!!!!!!!
Dawn from Newark, Delaware in the United States of America

I am Susie and would like to tell you guys, how much I am enjoying Joan Maguire's Books!! They are very enjoyable, and they are something that you do not ever want to put down!! I really enjoy these books; I can't wait until the next one that she puts out!!!!!!! I say go to your local book store, today and get one, you will not be disappointed!!!!!
Sue-from the United States of America

After reading through your range of books I felt I must compliment you Joan on the imaginative and entertaining way in which you presented each group and the Musicians in those groups. The way the stories were constructed is a credit to your work ethic. These must have taken considerable time to piece together and it is obviously a work of love for you.
I wish you all the success you truly deserve and look forward to seeing you next time you visit Tamworth.
Peter Harkins
Managing Director Cheapa Music
Country Music Capital Tamworth